T0114176

On this road

There are no signs

Saying caution

Sharp turn

Too fast

Causes overturn.

THE
BUMPS
IN
THE
ROAD

POEMS

Robert Swain Lewis

Order this book online at www.trafford.com
or email orders@trafford.com

Most Trafford titles are also available at major online book retailers.

Note for Librarians: A cataloguing record for this book is available from Library
and Archives Canada at www.collectionscanada.ca/amicus/index-e.html

Printed in the United States of America.

ISBN: 978-1-4251-1275-2 (sc)
ISBN: 978-1-4269-5762-8 (hc)

Trafford rev. 04/06/2011

 www.trafford.com

North America & international
toll-free: 1 888 232 4444 (USA & Canada)
phone: 250 383 6864 ♦ fax: 812 355 4082

I thank the Lord for protecting and keeping me safe through this difficult period in my life.

We have all experienced some bumps in the road.

Some of us have experienced financial setbacks, relationships that didn't work, loss of loved ones, and betrayal by friends.

It's not what you go through that makes you stronger.

It's the attitude which you embrace the bumps in the road, that makes you stronger.

CONTENTS

PART ONE

REFLECTING BACK

PART TWO

THE BUMPS IN THE ROAD

THE STREETS

PART FOUR

MY PRAYER

PART ONE

Reflecting Back

A Day Of Reflecting Back

We reflect back on this day,
To those who have departed...this way.
There is so much we think about
And even want to say.

Out of respect,
We bow our heads
And in silence pay,
Tribute to those
Who have gone home.
They were more
Than friends or foes,
To many of us
They were our heroes.

We remembered
The life they lived.
It is the joy and happiness
Of them that keep us fulfilled.

As this day comes to an end,
Whether you're
A relative or friend,
Your memories
Will remain with us
Until, we can be together again.

This poem is dedicated to

To the men and women

Of the Armed Forces,

Who gave their lives for this country.

WE SALUTE YOU ALL.

In Memory Of Rosa Parks

You are the cornerstone
Upon which the foundation is laid.
They all knew, once it started
There would be many days,
Those that followed would not be paid.

You were tired and refused to move.
You didn't worry about getting fired
Or the seat you would lose.
As if it was time to pick and choose,
Do what's right or continue to sing the blues.

In the background
Voices said,
Woman, do as you are told.
They didn't know
God was in control.
He gave you strength
To stand firm and bold.

I would liked to have seen
The look on their faces,
No disrespect intended,
You were just putting things in their places.

So, we salute you

Mother Rosa Parks.

You will always

Be remembered

In our hearts.

When There Was A Cause

You didn't stop
Or even pause.
You came together
For one cause,
With one mind
Knowing that you didn't
Have a lot of time.

You fought all day
And into the night.
Praying it would be alright
And hoping it would not last all night.

Some would pay
A heavier price than others.
When it was over and done,
You would be closer.
You would be united as one.

You didn't hesitate
To come to another's aid.
We saw some leaders born
And others made.

As the night faded away
And the day started
To show her face.
Hope was in place
And fate no longer delayed.

To those who fought
In the Civil Rights Movement,
THANK YOU.

To those who blood was shed and lives lost,
THANK YOU.

To those names that were never mentioned,
THANK YOU.

And to those that couldn't be there, whose prayers were with
them that marched,
THANK YOU.

To My Friend

I have seen your eyes
Filled with tears.
As you talked
About your mother,
From me to you
All of heaven
Is rejoicing with cheers.
Although,
I'm not a relative
I'm your brother.

Yes,
We miss the ones
Who are close to us.
Sometimes,
We want to give up.
You know,
Living afterward
Is really tough.

But life goes on, as it must
And the questioning stops
Without fuss.

Although,
She is not with you
In the natural,
She will always be
With you in spirit.

Remember the words
That she taught.
They can not be found
Nor brought.

The day will come
When both of you
Will be together,
Singing and praising God
Forever and ever.

Until, that day come
Stay prayerful
And in the word.
This will keep
The enemy on the run.

To my good friend,

In memory of your mother.

The day will come

When you'll see her again.

To Mr. P

It took four days
For you to show your face
In this...water up to the roof
No electric...horrible place.

If this had been in Texas
How long would it have taken
For you to go in with a plan laid?
You would stuck out your chest
Beat on it, as if by your powers
The people were saved.

Was it the people
Or the color of their skin?
I would hate to think
This cause you not
Not to follow the trend.

Where are the ex - Ps
That raised monies in the past?
These people need your help too
And they need it fast.

Now, we understand
Some of the problems
With your administration
No dedication and
Not enough human relations.

Consistency should be
A major quality for you
It's not good to leave people
Hungry and dirty
Sleeping on the curbs
And in the streets
Begging for someone
Anyone...to come.

So, the next time this happens
We hope you have a plan
Because you're suppose
To be the man, right?

Tears

We watched you shed tears
Behind them...
We heard the cheers of...
Hattie, Sidney, Louis, Denzel, Whoopi,
Cuba, and Halle
Saying, HERE, HERE,
As you stepped forward
There was no fear.

Few of us have been so honored
To received such an award.
You did not forget them
As you continued to march on.

We know you miss the person
Who taught you everything.
She is in heaven and
You're the song that she sings.

You made us proud, again
We walk with our heads high
Knowing that if we continue
To work hard and stay focus,
We can do more than just get by.

This poem is dedicated to JAMIE FOX

On winning the OSCAR AWARD

For the best actor in the movie

"RAY"

Now, America understands RAY CHARLES' life, music, and love.

Where Have They Gone?

They have all closed their eyes
They have all gone
To that great cloud
Beyond the sky.

Who will lead us
To that great prize?
I go to the place
Where you all are kept alive
And one day
I too, will rise.

I read the words
That you all wrote.
My eyes began to water
And my voice choke
And still,
It gives me faith and hope.

To know, that one day,
I'll be where you all are at
I pray my words be received,

Remembered and met
With inspiration
And great expectation.

And if it does
Not come fast,
I will not fret
As I continue
To wear many hats.

I know the day will come
When I'll hear in the background
All of your voices with cheers.

I will do my best
In this run
As we go
To the forefront.

So great ones of the past,
Your memories will live on
And it will forever last.

This poem is dedicated

To the Great Black Writers

Who have gone home.

Their words and lives

Will always be with us.

Why I Write

There is so much, I want to say
But, I must continue
To read the Word and pray.
People still try to entice me
Asking, can I come out and play?
I shake my head
Laugh and say...no way.

You see, I have been disappointed
In this life by many including,
The woman who claimed to be my wife.
The one that laid next to me in bed
And in the morning,
Breakfast she was fed.

I gave all I had
To the military,
The fast food industry,
And the hospital
Without mentioning any names
No one wanted to take the blame.

I was kicked to the curve
And mistreated
Each time, I was down
They thought, I was defeated.

Little did they know
This is part of the mission
That must be completed.

Writing gives me the chance
To express myself
And say wants on my mind.

So, I'll write about things
On my mind and in my heart.
I will write about love, hate,
And the wars that were fought.

But, most importantly,
I want to inspire and motivate
Others to keep their dream alive
And let everyone know
That in Christ is where you should abide.

As a child I was told
The pen is mightier
Than the sword.
You all will soon know
Because, I have just began to roar.

PART TWO

The Bumps In The Road

The Bumps In The Road

The bumps in this road
Are hard and cold.
Everyone is not allowed on it.
You must be mentally,
Physically, and spiritually fit
Or the bumps will cause you fits.

This road comes with a warning label
Be careful when riding
This is not just a fable.
Many have gotten on it
And thought they were able
But, as they went up and down
The ride had to be tabled.

On this road
There are no signs
Saying caution,
Sharp turn,
Too fast,
Causes overturn.

Some roads are gravel and dirt
You must maintain the right speed
Or the rocks will cause you hurt.

I have rode this road alone
Nothing to keep me
But a song.
Every once in a while
I come to a pothole
And go around,
Trying to avoid the pits falls
That could take me to the ground.

This road would be easy to take
If I had someone
That was real and fake.

Now, this is road easier to ride
Because the Lord is on my side
Off into the sunset, I'll glide
With the Lord's arms
Embracing me with a hold
Avoiding the bumps in the road.

I Have Been

I've been happy

And I've been sad

I've been up

And I've been down

I worked like a fool

And acted liked a clown

I took time out

To think on these things

It doesn't do any good

It just makes me mean.

This poem was entered into the

National Poetry Contest and won

The Editor's Choice Award in 2005.

Things In My Dreams

My dreams are not just dreams
They are filled with excitement,
Violence, and people that are mean.
I'm always hiding and on the run
From people chasing me with guns.

I don't know why
But I continue to stride.
I pace myself.
I can't do it alone.
I need a little help.

But help is nowhere in sight
And my day continues to be night.
I maintain faith and hope in my God
That one day soon it will be alright.

Some have asked what's wrong?
They seem sincere by their tone.
I don't know if they are ready to hear
Or will my words cause them to fear.

I will continue the pace that is sat
One day, I will wear only one hat.
I'm not worried about
My bank account being phat.
I just want to do God's will
And that's that.

I will fulfill the vision
And what has been said,
In heaven not hell
I will make my bed.

Now, that you know
A little more about me
Although it seems
These are some of the things in my dreams.

What If

What if,
I had never been born?
You know,
My heart would have never been torn.

What if,
I was blind and couldn't see,
Could I exist in this world
As we know it to be?

What if,
I couldn't hear,
Would my heart
Be filled with fear?

What if,
I couldn't walk,
And had to have help
Every where I go,
Would my words still be bold
Or would I do as I am told?

What if,
I couldn't feel,
Could I differentiate
The fake from the real?

What if,
I couldn't do all the above,
Would I still be accepted with a hug?
Would my head be in the sky
Or would it be low as people walked by?

I often wondered,
What if?

Don't Blame Me

Why do you blame me?
Is it the color of my skin that you see
Or the man that you'll never be?
I'm no different than you or he
The same color blood in you is in me.

You know, I too am free
Why can't you leave me alone
And let me be?
Remember,
You came and got me.

I did nothing to offend you.
I've been accused and beaten
Till I'm blue.
And even in today's time
It's hard to have peace of mind.

You will not let the past go
Remember, you reap what you sow.

Now, I'm tired and want to rest
Don't you think I've passed the test?
I want to enjoy life
And the American dream
Raise my family in a nice home
You know what I mean.

I am totally free.
Why don't you get over it
And stop blaming me.

The Truth Will Come Out

Two weeks have come and gone
I'm still wondering what went wrong.

Has not had much rest
Did what I thought was best.

Life has not always
Been good to me in the past,
Should have went slow instead of fast.

Was I wrong to re-hire? Maybe!
Should have used my authority to fire.

I tried to assist and help
But some would not accept.

I see some them in the streets
They say hi,
The look on my face ask...why?

Now, I'm on the outside looking in.
In their minds...they win.
But, I'm a fighter through thick and thin.

Just wait and see because
The truth will come out in the end.

They Left Me For Dead

They gave me up
And left me for dead
Told me to go somewhere
Else to be feed.

They took away my keys
Which knocked me
To my knees
As I was down there
I said, Lord, again
Why me?

Never in my wildest dream
Could any three be so mean
In my mind,
They liked me or though it seem.

Now,
You must be wondering
What's going on in my head
No job,
No money,
But, well read.

Started to make a sign that said,
I don't usually stand
On the corner and beg.

Instead, I asked the Lord
To help me and give me strength
To forgive those that left me for dead.

This was not a physical death
but a financial death.

All three time,
they took my keys away.

There were many times
I didn't know how
I was going to make it.

But God was with me.

Men In Power

I've seen men in great power
Misusing their authority
Until the last hour
Look you in the face sour.

Look at you like, you're the cause
Let the truth be known
They didn't have the galls
They ran and hid their faces
So it couldn't be shown.

These are the men in high places
You must be careful
They will laugh and grin with you
Later, ask you to tie their shoe laces.

After the laugh and grin
You ask, what....who?
Their look...says you.

They have pen-house suites
On the 13th floor of the tower
You can't get to them
But, they can get to you
These are the men in power.

Black Men Do Cry: Part I

Last night,
I cried,
Wondering,
How I was going to get by.
This is nothing new for me
I cry night and day
You see.

D H S on me
Because of child-support.
I went to school
Got an education
Instead of playing sports.

I'm suppose to be strong black man
And stand up straight.
Am I a fool or just bait?

As a child, I was told
BOY, when you walk
Down the street,
Hold your head high.

Now that I'm older, it bores me
Who can I turn to?
And where is she, when I'm in need?

Instead of spreading my troubles around
I did the best thing, I got on my knees
With my face to the ground
And prayed to the Almighty above
Don't look on me as others do
Look on me with love.

You see, I don't need a lot
Just a chance and
And every once-in-a-while...a hug.

Now, I don't mind crying in front of you
Because, this is how, I stay true
And it has nothing to do with
Getting touch with the other side
Because if I don't show it
Inside, it will hide.

So, that old saying
Black men don't cry
Don't believe the hype
Because that's a lie.

Black Men Do Cry: Part II

WE CRY,
When we are wrongfully jailed
And have to spend half of our life
Behind bars in a cell.

WE CRY,
When we have the necessary education
And requirements to get ahead
To take care of our families without beg
Sometimes denied, but
We continue to stand on two legs.

WE CRY,
When it says on the application
Check here if convicted of a crime
We are honest and check yes
And still doing time.

WE CRY,
When we go to the store
And a dollar short.
It's like being stabbed
Again, in the heart.

WE CRY,
When we have to catch the bus
Because we can't afford a car.
The transit is what we trust
After a while,
Riding seems not too long and far.

WE CRY,
When we are passed over for promotion
Because of the color of our skin.
As if by nature
We are cursed...hum
What is the sin?

I Have Seen

I have seen mountains so high
That it reaches the sky.
I have seen valleys so low
I had nowhere else to go.

It has rain so hard on me
If it rain any harder, I will bleed.
I have seen it snow so deep
Until, I couldn't go out and take a peep.

I have seen it so cold and wonder,
How could people be that bold?
I have seen all type of weather in my life
Some hot and some cold as ice.

I asked,
What is this I'm going through?
A voice responded
You're chosen of the few.
Every one can not eat this food
Because it's something many can not chew.

My faith will not
Let me be defeated.
I take the good with the bad
Walk with my head up
And not be sad.

Like the Apostle Paul,
I have learned to be content
With whatever state I'm in.
Everything on the other side
Is not all green.
This is some of what I've seen.

Thorns In My Side

This pain,
I can't explain
It has no name
Make a man almost go insane
Tried to understand
What's going on
I don't know
Only that my heart
Has been disappointed and torn.

I wish it was over and done
You know, I'm ready to enjoy life
And have a little fun
And stop this long run.

Something inside says
It's not time yet
Stay on the road
And you will not regret.

I concluded,
That I will rise
Live and not hide
From the thorns in my side.

Not Guilty

I did nothing wrong
Just followed in the footsteps
Of those that sat the tone.

I gave it my best
Worked longer and harder than the rest
No disrespect intended
To those before and after me.
But, this is how I got to the top, you see.

I went, when I couldn't any further
Growing up was hard for some us
Without a father or brother.

Society stamped me with approval
And took me to the pinnacle of life.
Now, it seeks my removal.

I can feel in my back, the knife
But, I hold fast to my faith
When it's over, I will not hate.

I am innocent of this charge
Just took life as society gave me
And lived large.

Trapped

I feel trapped and all alone
I've been kicked off my throne.
Now, I'm singing an old song
Where is home?

I have nowhere to go,
And nothing to show,
Nowhere to run.
Are my days over
Of having fun?

Who can help me?
The one I chose
Is the one I lose.

I feel like I'm trapped
In a desert without a map
Seems like no way out.

I keep faith and hope alive.
My enemies' steps are numbered,
As I continue to strive.
And one day soon,
Above them I will rise.

PART THREE

The Streets

The Streets Are Calling Me

I here the streets
Calling my name.
On every corner and
Stop light it's the same.

The streets are crying out to me
Come, look, and see.
We have what you need,
Out here is where you can be free.

I answered the street and said,
If I accept your offer,
In hell and not heaven,
I'll make my bed.

The benefits of the streets
Does not last long.
One day you're here
The next day you're gone.

But that's not all,
In the streets, everyone is looking
To have a ball at another's expense,
Running around like headless chickens
Without any sense.

Therefore, I will decline this offer
And never mention it to me again.
I will not go back and commit this great sin
In Christ is where I can be free
When the streets...call me.

Those Days

I've had good days

And I've had bad days

I've worked long and hard

What did it pay?

I've walked in the light

And I've walked in the dark

Always a fight

Always a bark.

The Game

Don't hate the player
Get in the game.

This is where you find
Wealth and fame.

Life as you know it
Will not be the same.

Many have gone on
Under another name.

Do what you must
To remain.

No matter what happens
Under your reign.

One thing remains constant
And that's the game.

The ole' saying
"Don't hate the player
Hate the game".

I changed that to:

"Don't hate the player
Get in the game".

The game does not change
Only the players change.

Papa

Papa was not a rolling stone.
He was the only stone rolling.
Papa knocked down more women
Than you could with pins bowling.

At early age
Papa left home,
In search of
The American dream.
Only to find life
In the streets so mean.

Papa was a bad dude.
He dressed nice
And looked good.
Many admired him
As he knew they would.

Sometimes papa was sweet
Sometimes rude,
Took pictures of women
With clothes on
And in the nude.

As Papa got older
He began to change.
He said, nothing last forever
And things never stay the same.

Although many admired
The things I've done,
Don't follow in my steps.
I have jumped out of many windows
And came face to face with guns.

As Papa looked back on his life,
He remembered having
A woman in every town.
But, the smile on his face soon leaves
Because he recall hiding in brushes
And behind trees.

Now, Papa has a beautiful wife
And a nice home, those days are over
When Papa was the only stone rolling.

I KNEW PAPA...ONCE.

Jack Of All: Master Of None

I played basketball
And was good.
You know what's funny?
I had the skills
But the court
I could not feel.

Baseball was my first love
But it was only a tip
Of what was to come from above.

I was so good at pool
I should have been on T.V.
So every one could see
Ever time I walked in
It was time for school.

I bank all eight
While others shot straight.
Some stayed late
Cause they didn't
Understand the rules.

I played pin-pong
Switching hands
And turning around
Slamming the ball
That almost burst.

When it hit the floor,
King Tutt, Big C, and Richie Rich
Didn't have a chance
Just an itch.

Big Lucas and I
Were two of a kind.
We beat everyone in spades
Because it was our time.

We had what it took
To rack up books after books.
People came from far and near
Knowing their eyes
Would be filed with excitement
And mesmerized by the words they would hear.

In the conclusion of it all,
What would be said?
Was I the Jack of all
And Master of none
Or did I live life to be the fulness
And had too much fun?

Whatever is said,
In the mornings,
I always made my bed.

My Brother, Why?

We took the same oaths and vows
Ten years later,
I'm still shaking my head
Asking how?

You're suppose to be my brother
But, you betrayed me like the others.
After I told my mother
I'm coming home and that's where I went.
You moved all of my furniture
Into your girlfriend's apartment.

You lied to my face
About moving my furniture
From the storage space.
You should have been honorable
And told the truth
Because that's what I expected from you.

Now, I know why
You could not look
Me in my eyes.
All this time
It was nothing but lies.

Stay-At-Home-Dad

My, how the times have changed
With modern technology
And intervention
Nothing stays the same.

Your wife is off to work
And babies at home
Needing to be feed.
I can't believe
You a stay-at-home-dad.

She's bringing all the money in,
You at home,
It ought to be a sin.
After she get home
Her bath water and food
Should be ready,
But the only thing on your mind
Is her calling you daddy.

When she wakes up in the mornings,
Breakfast should be prepared,
And not worry about making the bed,
After all....you're
A stay-at-home-dad.

So, how does it feel?
Do you think, you're king of the hill?
You don't pay any of the bills
At home all day with a glass on chill.

If I was you,
I would not be so carefree.
One day, you may come home
And find your few things in the street.

This has nothing to do with
What goes on in bed,
It's because, you're
A STAY-AT HOME-DAD.

If Men Could Have A Baby

If men could have a baby
They would understand
What it's like during certain
Months and times of the year
To be lazy.

In the middle of the night
Demand ice cream and chips
And drive the other crazy.

Gaining weight would not be an issue
Because men would not want to hide
Behind closed doors
And use tissues.

If the roles were reversed
Could men handle the pain?
Or would they go insane
Trying to kill the pain?

So men, watch the words you say

Let her know, she's the one you prefer

Treat your woman like a lady

Because this would not happen

If men could have a baby.

You're Right, You're Not A Role Model

How can you say
You're not a role model?
In the locker room
You want everyone to follow
On the court
You do nothing but holla.

Maybe,
They should get you a bottle
Because, you're right
You're not a role model.

I agree with you,
Parents should be the one
Who their children look up to
But, how do you explain
When they buy your jerseys and shoes?

Kids look up to you
To some degree
On the court
When they see
Your all around play
They too believe.

Until, you open your mouth

And began to shout

Here it comes again

So everyone look out.

No More

I don't want to look no more
At the things I did before.
It's amazing,
When I think about it
I become bored.

These things are in the past
They are tempo
Because it didn't last.

I'm running toward the future
Trying not to go too fast.
I don't want to do things half-half.

The past is the past
Out of mind, at last.
I'm going through a new door
And remembering, the past no more.

Temptations

Temptations are nothing but temptations
You can become trapped
And lose your patience.

Something comes along
And tempts you
It's not real
Nor is it true.

This tempter wants to enter your mind
And take all of your time
It blows you away
You want to leave
But you stay.

What is this mystical power
That has you soaring
Leaps and bounds
And upon towers?

Life is no good without relations
You can make it
If you endure the temptation.

I Will Not Go Back

No food on the table

No money coming in

Where are they that spoke

Saying, stay faithful

And you will win?

Adversary tempting me

To commit sin.

I avoid them

Because I will not bend

Nor will I follow the trend.

I will not give in

This I vowed

Until the end.

Never Wanted To

I never wanted to
Share with you my pain.

What do you get out of it?
What is your gain?

When you go through
And I go through
It's not the same.

We are here for a reason.
It will come forth
In the right season.

But until then,
Remain steadfast,
And in the end
We both shall win.

Remember,
No one was frame
And no one is the blame.

Be careful,
After it's over,
Your mind and heart
Will be tamed.

Are you ready
To carry a different name
Without going insane?

I don't think so because
This is my life and my pain.

Decisions

Through out our time,

We have made decisions

In hope that it will shine.

Some right and some wrong

As a child and adult grown

All were meant to help.

Drove and picked up people

Didn't ask for anything except,

Do unto others

What has been shown to you

And never think of yourself

Better than anyone else.

Dreams Do Come True

What started
As a thought,
Over a period of time
Becomes your heart.

You try to explain it
To those who are close.
Sometimes it's rejected
By friends and other folks.

You continue on
And don't give up.
If only you had been born
With a golden spoon and cup.

This is the normal process
When it's over, said, and done,
Those that didn't believe
Will confess.

Never look back
Continue forward
Without slack
Stay on the road
And you will have much success.

Stay focus or people will spend

A life time, asking you,

What happened?

Dreams do come true.

I Am Who I Am

The time has come
For me to face the music.
I must walk and not run
Lay aside the cannon
And the gun.
This does not mean
Give up life and
Stop having fun.

My life can not be changed
Do I have a say
Who becomes my wife?
Am I ready to take the reign?

I will accomplish many things.
Do I have enough fingers
To wear the rings?
It may upset and offend
Those who say they understand
But don't want to bend.

I did not come to this
Conclusion on my own.
It has been predicted
And many have known.
One day, I will rise
And take my stand
To be God's leading man.

This I do in low key
Not looking for gifts or a fees.
All this will happen without a bam
Because I am who I am.

PART FOUR

My Prayer

My Prayer

Father, I thank thee this day

For protecting me,

Keeping me safe,

And holding back the danger

That could have come my way.

This is the day that you have created

Blessed and set aside.

Because Christ die

For the sins of the world,

And in you is where I abide.

Now Lord, give me strength

To take back what is mine.

This is now and this is the time

For me to come forward and be bold

To proclaim the good news

As it was foretold.

Your Man

Lord, in your presence I stand
Trying to do the best I can.
Instill, in me thy Holy Spirit
That I will become the man
Who you are calling for this day.
Let my eyes stay on you
Instead of the pay.

Lord, I serve you with all my might
Because your word said,
Walk by faith and not by sight.
Although, it's dark in my life
It will not last all night.

In you, I put all of my trust
Which allow me to handle
The confusion and the fuss.

Let thy Holy Spirit
Give me what to say.
Here this prayer Lord,
In Jesus' name, I pray.

Lord, Help Me

Lord, help me
To do your will
Hold back the enemy
And all of their ills.

I'm trying to run this race.
Let thy Holy Spirit set the pace.
If I go too fast or too slow
Then shall thy Holy Spirit
Let me know.

I want to live a life
That will shine.
And tell everyone
Over here, you too
Can have a good time.

Safe On The Road

Lord, I thank you
For keeping me
Safe on this road.

Even though,
The car tried to run
Hot and cold.

But, thy Holy Spirit said,
"Do as you are told"
So, I rebuked the enemy
And stood bold on your word.

Because your word will not fold
Thank you Lord,
For keeping me safe on this road.

Lord, I Thank You

Lord, I thank you this day

For the blessings

That have come my way,

Anoint my mouth

That I will know

What to say,

To those

Who are struggling

To survive

From day to day.

Fifteen Years Ago

It has been fifteen years
Since I faced
The beginning of
My worse fears.

Fifteen years ago,
I was kicked out
No job,
No money,
Just broke.

No car,
To get around
Rode a bike
Looking for a job
Throughout town.

Fifteen years ago,
I was cold and hungry
With nowhere to go
Yet, maintained hope
That one day,
It would pass away.

Fifteen years ago,
The woman I loved
Looked me in my eyes
Had no pity, as she
Took my children
To another city.

I gave her everything
Including the kitchen sink
As she stood with her lawyer
Looking me up and down
Didn't even blink
But turned around
As she walked through
The door and winked.

I went through fifteen years of hell
It seemed like I was behind bars
In a cell,
Without bail.

Fifteen years later,
The same folks
That kick me,
Trick me,
Believed in me,
Wrote a letter, saying
Now, you're free.

Fifteen years later,
The same folk
Who held me down
With my face to the ground
When I tried to smile
But only frown.

They gave me
Both of their hands
Saying, we want you
Today, right now
To lead and be the man.

And now, the time has come
As I look back
And see where God
Has brought me from
No longer am I hiding
And on the run.

Now, stronger than ever
Is my faith and hope
In the almighty
As I reflect back
On fifteen years ago.

Robert Lewis was born and raised in Cincinnati, Ohio.

He is a military veteran.

Robert graduated from Cameron University in Lawton, Oklahoma, with B.S. in Criminal Justice, B.A. in Political Science, and a Masters degree in Public Administration from the University of Oklahoma.

At the time this book was being published, Robert was employed by the state of Oklahoma with the Department of Human Services. He continues to work for the state of Oklahoma, but with the Office of Juvenile Affairs.